The Glacialists' Magazine: A Monthly Magazine Of Glacial Geology

F. H. Butler Publisher

In the interest of creating a more extensive selection of rare historical book reprints, we have chosen to reproduce this title even though it may possibly have occasional imperfections such as missing and blurred pages, missing text, poor pictures, markings, dark backgrounds and other reproduction issues beyond our control. Because this work is culturally important, we have made it available as a part of our commitment to protecting, preserving and promoting the world's literature. Thank you for your understanding.

AUGUST, 1893.

Vol. 1. No. 1. Price 6d.

The Glacialists' MAGAZINE.

A Monthly Magazine of Glacial Geology.

EMBODYING THE PROCEEDINGS OF THE GLACIALISTS' ASSOCIATION.

EDITED BY
PERCY F. KENDALL, F.G.S.,
Lecturer on Geology at the Yorkshire College,
And Secretary of the British Association Committee on Erratic Blocks;

ASSISTED BY
WARREN UPHAM, F.G.S.A.,
Assistant on the Geol. Surveys of New Hampshire, Minnesota, and the United States;

C. E. DE RANCE, F.G.S., F.R.G.S.,
Of H.M. Geol. Survey; President of the Glacialists' Association;

AND

J. LOMAS, A.R.C.S.

CONTENTS:

		Page.
1.	Introductory	1
2.	Presidential Address to the Glacialists' Association, 1893. By C. E. De Rance	2
3.	On an Intrusive Mass of Boulder Clay. By A. R. Dwerryhouse	9
4.	Back Proceedings of the Glacialists' Association	12
5.	Review. Howorth; The Glacial Nightmare and the Flood	15
6.	Notes	20
7.	Current Glacial Bibliography	24
8.	July Meeting of the Glacialists' Association	28

LONDON: F. H. BUTLER, 158, BROMPTON ROAD, S.W.

THE GLACIALISTS' MAGAZINE.

A MONTHLY MAGAZINE OF GLACIAL GEOLOGY.

Vol. 1. No. 1.   AUGUST, 1893.   Price 6d.

INTRODUCTORY.

THE Glacialists' Association had its origin in a meeting called to consider the desirability of organising a systematic investigation of the but little studied erratics of the eastern parts of Lancashire and Cheshire. The meeting, more ambitious than its convener, enrolled itself under the title of the "North-West of England Boulder Committee," and enlarged its purview so as to include "all observations relating to the glacial phenomena of the western watershed of England, Wales, and of the Isle of Man." Meetings were held monthly, at first, for the purpose of organisation, and later to hear and discuss reports and papers. These meetings were held in succession at many different places within the area defined by the rules. The first batch of reports submitted to the British Association Committee on Erratic Blocks made up nine-tenths of the whole number recorded by that Committee in 1891, and was contributed by 16 members.

At the first annual meeting it was decided, in view of the accession of members from districts outside the area defined by the rules, to alter the name of the organisation to the more catholic one of "The Glacialists' Association," and to enlarge its scope so as to include the observation of all glacial phenomena. The meetings have been held in many towns in the North and West of England, one in the Isle of Man, and one in Edinburgh. The investigation of the distribution of erratics was continued and the members of the Association contributed to the twentieth report of the Committee on Erratic Blocks about nineteen-twentieths of the whole number recorded. The completion of the second year of the existence of the Association has left its Council in possession of a number of valuable papers, some supplying details of the glacial geology of small districts, and others raising questions of great general interest, and the Committee has had to decide in what form they should be placed on record.

A monthly Magazine has been adopted as being best adapted to the needs of the Association, and a hope is entertained that it may prove of interest to all geologists who devote time to the study of the most striking episode in the whole range of the history of our hemisphere.

The Magazine is commenced upon a modest scale, but if, as the Editors venture to anticipate, it receives the support of glacialists on both sides of the Atlantic, it will be possible to increase the size and make a more liberal use of illustrations. Negotiations are already in progress to secure the co-operation of a distinguished American glacialist.

The space at present available will be allotted to—(1) Brief abstracts of the back proceedings of the Glacialists' Association; (2) Papers *in extenso* from the same source; (3) Notes on the progress of Glacial Geology; (4) Reviews *signed* or *initialled*; (5) Correspondence; (6) Abstract of the last meeting of the Glacialists' Association, and notice of the next; (7) Bibliography.

Presidential Address.
(*Delivered 19th March,* 1892.)

By C. E. DE RANCE, Esq., F.G.S., F.R.G.S., F.R.Met.S., Assoc.I.C.E.,
of H.M. Geol. Survey.

In the spring of 1875, the Lords of the Admiralty sent out an expedition under Captain Nares, " to attain the highest northern latitude, and, if possible, to reach the North Pole." No geologist was appointed to accompany the same, but the then Director-General of the Geological Survey was requested to order one of his staff to instruct the two naturalists of the expedition in Geological Surveying, and the choice of the late Sir Andrew Ramsay fell upon myself, I presume from my having published in *Nature* (Vol. XI., pp. 447, 467, 492, and 508), an abstract of what was then known of the geology of the Arctic regions.

In 1878, it fell to my lot to work up the geological results obtained, which were communicated, in association with Colonel Feilden, the Senior Naturalist to the Geological Society of London, the British Association, and formed an appendix of Captain Sir George Nares' "Voyage to the Polar Sea."

From these and subsequent studies, it appears to me that it may be useful for me to examine how far the results obtained in these northern climes throw light on the glacial conditions which have visited Europe and America, and how far they support or negative certain theories which have lately been strongly supported by Sir Robert Ball, F.R.S.

The Nares expedition brought back 60 species of Palæozoic fossils, those of Silurian age ranging from the lower to the upper division, Llandeilo and Wenlock type being present. Mollusca, Crustacea, and large corals were well represented, the facies being rather more American than European.

Dr. Conybeare appears to have been the first to realise that English Upper Silurian forms reappeared in the Artic Regions (*Brit. Assoc. Report*, 1832), and Mr. Salter was the first to recognise that though species found at Wenlock, Dudley, and in Gothland occur in the Arctic Silurians, that the facies is rather American than European. The Upper Silurian of Grinnel Land was first determined by Professor Meek, on specimens collected by Dr. Hayes, and they were found by the *Polaris* Expedition in Hall Land on the opposite side of the Straits, and correspond to forms occurring in the New York Catskill series.

The Devonian Hamilton series and Genesee States of the United States reappear on the Mackenzie River, between Clearwater River and the Arctic Ocean, and these contain brine springs and petroleum, extending continuously from Rock Island, Illinois, to the Arctic Sea, a distance of 2,500 miles, containing the same fauna. They point to a wide uniformity of conditions in old Palæozoic times.

Of newer age than these rocks, are coal bearing lower carboniferous rocks, first discovered by Parry in the group of islands named after him, the fossils resemble the Irish Calp Series, and those of the Eifel. These rocks are well developed in Bear Island, and were named the "Ursa Stage" by Prof. O. Heer, who pointed out the occurrence in it of *Stigmaria ficoides*, and other well known European forms, and that the assemblage closely corresponded to the Yellow Sandstones of Kiltorkan, and the lower carboniferous flora of Russia. It is worthy of note that this was the first rich flora of the Earth's history, and that it occupied both what are now temperate and arctic zones, in the Old World and the New, pointing to wide spread continental conditions under a uniform climate. The leaves of the evergreen tree *Lepidodendron* are as fully developed in the Arctic regions as in the south of Ireland and the Vosges.

The subsidence in Europe that brought about the growth of extensive coral reefs in mountain limestone sea, equally affected the Arctic regions. Lieut. Anjou, and officers of the Russian Navy, discovered Lias fossils in New Siberia, described by Wrangel; later Sir Edward Belcher, in 1885, discovered the Lias resting at a height of 570 feet, on the carboniferous limestone, on Exmouth Island (77° N. lat., and 98° W. long.), containing an *Icthyosaurus*, according to Owen, closely allied to the *I. acutus* of the Whitby Lias. The carboniferous limestones below were covered with *Spirifer Keilhovii*, and a *Zaphrentis*; beneath the limestone was soft sandstone dipping at a low angle, probably referable to the Ursa stage. Similar sections, sequence, and fossils were later discovered by M'Clintock, Sherard Osborne, at Prince Patrick's Island and Eglinton Island, which latter yielded *Ammonites*. The Lias is also well represented in Spitzbergen. *Jurassic* marles, brown coal, and shell-breccias rest on crystalline rocks in East Greenland, with *Goniomya v-scripta*, *Rhynchonella fissicostata*, Suess, *Myacites*, and *Ostrea*, as in the Middle Dogger of Yorkshire and the Western Isles, the brown coal occurs with the Rynchonella, a characteristic Rhætian form. The Jurassics of the East coast of Kuhn Island contain *Aucella concentrica* in five varieties, all of which occur in the Russian Jurassics from the Lower Volga to the mouth of the Petshorva. *Aucella Mosquensis* occurs in the Oolites of Spitzbergen, which overlie the Lias containing *Hybodus* and *Icthyosaurus*, and attains a thickness of 1,200 feet at Mount Agardh.

The Cretaceous rocks are well represented on the west coast of Greenland, on the south side of the Noursoak Peninsula, and the north coast of Disco Island, where the oldest beds occur, called the "Kome Beds" by Heer; they reach 1,000 feet, and lie in undulating hollows in the Gneiss, they contain lignites, and the beautiful cycads—*Zamites arcticus, Glozzozamites Hogenggeri*, which occurs, according to Heer, in the Urgonian strata of Wernsdorff. These beds do not, apparently, occur in America, but the newer "*Atane* strata" of Heer contain the leaves of dicotyledonous plants, as *Magnolia alternans*, Heer, and may be linked with the Dakota strata, and constitute a "limit flora," as is the case with the European Gault, in which dicotyledons first appear. The Cretaceous rocks in America occupy 80,000 square miles in the Missouri valley alone; the Dakota beds occur at the base, and are overlaid by beds corresponding to the English Grey Chalk, with marine fossils.

The Tertiary deposits of America indicate tropical conditions, fan-palms abounding, which were absent from Cretaceous flora, that preceded the American marine Cretaceous beds. Each successive flora indicates more temperate conditions, and the last of them corresponds with the Tertiary flora discovered in the Arctic regions, first found by Sir Charles Giesecke in 1821, at Disco Island, where two horizons of lignites and plant-bearing beds are separated by 2,000 feet of basalts. Subsequently these beds were discovered in Jan Mayen Island, Spitzbergen, and in Francis Joseph Land, where brown coals occur

The Spitzbergen series is 1,500 feet thick, contains brown coal also, 26 insects, and many plants, and a marine band containing *Ditrupa incrassata*, which occurs at Barton Hampshire, and *Terebratula grandis* of the English Crags. Amongst the plants is a lime (*Tilia Walmeni*), a juniper, an arborvita, two Spitzbergen species were found by Lieut. Payer in the Germanica mountains, Sabine Island, East

Greenland, viz.:—*Taxodium distichum* and *Populus Arctica*. Firs and poplars grow 15° further north than plane-trees, so that, assuming planes to have had their northern limit in 79° N., the fir may have grown, if there was land there, as far north as the Pole, and beds of similar character re-appear on the Asiatic and North American coasts. Of 30 plants in the Grinnel Land Tertiaries, 18 occur in Spitzbergen, and indicate a somewhat colder condition than the Disco Island beds, 11° further south. Six of the Grinnel Land flora occur in Europe, one of these, *Pinus abies*, now never ranges north of $69\frac{1}{2}$° N. lat. The Greenland beds contain the Japanese genera *Glyptostrobus* and *Thujopsis*; it is worthy of note that *T. Europœus* occurs in the Baltic amber, and at Armissan (Narbonne), associated with American forms in both cases, as pointed out by Professor Göppert. As Œningen also occur four palms of American types, and the conifers *Sequoia* and *Taxodium*. Palms, both of American and African types, are absent in advancing northwards, as are the bones of long-armed apes, present in the Miocenes of Central Europe.

The Grinnel Land Tertiaries contain the Norway spruce (*Pinus abies*), *Populus arctica*, and two species of birch, one of them of very large size, Viburnum, water-lilies, and a water beetle. The Grinnel Land Tertiary strata rise to a height of 1,000 feet above the sea, and are there overlaid by fine mud and glacial drift, with shells of *Saxicava rugosa*, *Astarte*, and *Mya truncata*, now living in the adjacent sea-bed. Stems of two species of *Laminaria* in the mud beds occur up to 200 feet above the sea, and retain their sea-shore odour, pointing to the recentness of the elevation of that amount. In Grinnel Land no ice-cap occurs, and glaciers are few, and none descend to the sea-level north of 81°, while the opposite coast of Hall Land is smothered, the ice-cap hanging over cliffs of Silurian Limestone 1,100 feet high, and falling in avalanches, with rocks torn from the cliffs on to the floe-bergs below.

The destructive force exercised upon rocks during the progress of expansion is a most potent factor in Polar regions, and there is nothing comparable with it in temperate climes. On the first sign of thaw large masses of rock separate at the planes of weakness formed by joints and bedding, and become detached from the sides of the deep gullies, or "rakes," which seam and scar the cliffs, and act as channels for the passage of the frost-worn material above to the "screes" concealing the base of the cliffs below. At the close of transient summer, the cleaved slate cliffs, the harder rocks, and the loose material forming the screes, are alike charged with water, no transition takes place, and, in a moment, without warning, the Arctic winter converts moisture and running water into ice, which expanding, shivers the rocks, the fragments of which remain bound by ice until the next following warm episode doing duty for an Arctic summer.

The "Ice-foot" is built up not so much of frozen sea-water, as of drifted autumn snows, masking the screes, which coming in contact with sea-water below the freezing point of fresh water, is instantaneously converted into a vertical wall of solid ice, which extends upwards from the sea margin, and increases in height as the snow falls, and is welded in by splashes of sea water from below. In Smith's Sound, in sweeping curves and deeper bays it is 100 yards in breadth, but absent from exposed and projected headlands. When the "season floe," or young ice first forms, there is little difference between the level of the floe and the ice-foot, but the former steadily increases in height, and the latter daily oscillates with the tide, so that a junction never takes place.

When the solar rays first exert their force, the snow lying on the screes near the ice-foot is first melted, the dark Talus absorbs heat, and a deep trench is formed which fills with fresh water, which makes its way through transverse gulleys to the sea at low tide, through which the sea water rushes on the return, and passing east and west, re-assorts the materials in the gulleys, which form a species of old sea margins; these are found in sheltered places, at all heights up to 300 feet, where, of course, wave action is impossible, proving the gradual rise of the land. These upland terraces are largely destroyed by summer torrents which make their way to the sea-margin, and there the stone-laden in-floes, which mingle their contents with the shells living in the surrounding waters. These form in sheltered bays, outside which the irresistible pressure of the Polar Pack throws up the soft material into a bar, the bay becomes a lake, until upheaval allows the water to cut a passage to the sea, the lake is emptied, and countless shells strew the surface of the mud, and are together transported by stream action to lower levels. The rock surface between gaps in the terraces, old and new, is invariably glaciated by pebbles included in the bottom of sea-ice, which, in hummocks eight to fifteen thick, grinds up and down with the action of the tide, making a well marked and peculiar sound.

Dr. Sutherland in 1853 described precisely the same phenomena or Cornwallis and Beechey Islands, in Barrow Straits, west of Lancaster Sound, Arctic sea shells occurring with travelling erratics, in old beeches up to 1,000 feet above the sea.

In Greenland the glaciers often cling to land beneath the sea, to a distance of three miles, after they have passed beyond the coast-line, until the buoyant property of water upon ice comes into operation, the daily rise and fall of the tide produces a hinge-like action, detaching huge ice islands, sometimes 200 feet above water and two miles in length. Dr. Sutherland calculates that taking the density of basalts as 2·5, and that of ice as 0·92, that an iceberg of 200 feet high above water, a mile long, and half a mile broad, could carry 140 million tons of rocky material.

Admiral Nares thus describes the difference between an ordinary floe-berg and the Polar Pack : " The former, composed of ice about six feet in thickness, on meeting with an obstruction is torn in pieces as it presses past it ; the latter, some 80 or 100 feet thick, forces its way past any impediment which may be in its course, without damage to itself . . . . nipping against the heavy floe-bergs lining the coast, some of them 40 feet in height, and many thousand tons in weight, tilting them over one after another, and forcing them higher up the shore, without receiving the slightest harm itself, not a piece breaking away. The constant impact of these masses leaves series of banks of mud and gravel mounds parallel to the coast. At Cape Union, Nares estimated the thickness of the Polar Pack at 80 feet, Scoresby at Spitzbergen 26 feet, Sir J. Parry at Melville Island 42 feet, Sir Robert M'Clure at Banks Land 78 feet, Sir Robert Collins in Behring Straits 42 feet, and Dr. Kane in Smith's Sound 60 feet. Floe-bergs pile up on the beach to 60 feet in height, many of them weighing 30,000 tons each, and form a rampart 200 yards in width, of solid ice.

The furthest north reached by Parry in 1823, was in Spitzbergen, 82° 45′ N., that of Commander Markham and Lieut. Parr was 83° 20′ 26″ N., on the 12th May, 1876; the temperature of the air was 8° F., that of the surface of the sea, 28·5° F., of the bottom of the sea, 28·8 F., the depth of the sea was 72 fathoms, with a clay bottom, the probable set of the tides N.W.—S.E., the thickness of the ice was 64 inches; small crustaceans of two species abounded at the sea bottom; traces of the Arctic hare were met with 23 miles from land.

Summarizing these results, it would appear that variations of climate were unknown until the beginning of the Upper Cretaceous period, after which a slow process of refrigeration commenced.

That there is no evidence of former glacial periods in the Arctic area; and it is probable that the period of cold commenced in the Arctic regions during, or shortly before, the advent of cold further south.

That the mud deposits extending up to 1,000 feet in the extreme north, with perfect bivalve shells and stems of *laminanaria*, do not correspond to the Glacial Drift of the British Isles, except as regards the Clyde Beds.

An Intrusive Mass of Boulder Clay at Bidston, Cheshire.
By ARTHUR R. DWERRYHOUSE.
(Read 4th June, 1892.)

The section was exposed during the operations in connection with a house lately completed for Mr. R. H. Hudson, situated on the western slope of Bidston Hill, a little to the south of the Upton Road. The cutting was in a fir plantation on the opposite (eastern) side of Vyner Road. The cutting has since been filled up, and its site is occupied by the carriage drive to the aforementioned house.

The surface at this point is 102 feet above Ordnance Datum, and the dip of the strata is 5° S.

The beds through which the section passes have been let down by two north and south faults which hade towards each other, forming a trough, and having a throw of at least six feet.

The rocks exposed are the Keuper Basement Beds (Fig. 3 of the survey), and the Upper Bunter (Fig. 3), there being between them a bed of bluish white marl, which averages six feet in thickness. The marl has been let down by the faults already mentioned, and the present surface of the land being below the original level of the marl, that between the faults is the only portion remaining (Fig. 3).

The section Fig. 1 runs east and west, and that in Fig. 2, north and south.

The surface soil (1. Fig. 1) is scanty, very sandy, and of a dark greyish brown colour.

The Keuper (2) overlying the marl band consists of a greyish black sandstone, probably owing its colour to vegetable matter. This is in some parts much broken up and attains a maximum thickness of four feet on the northern face and five feet on the southern.

The marl band consists of four distinct layers:—An upper columnar bed (3) in which the marl is cracked into rough columns about half an inch to an inch in diameter, the joints being stained red. An upper stratified bed (4), which shows no columnar structure, and in which there are thin horizontal layers of yellow sandy marl. A lower columnar bed (5) similar to (3), and a lower stratified bed (6) similar to (4).

The lowest bed visible consists of a hard greyish red sandstone, locally known as an iron band, which I take to be the hard bed which usually forms the uppermost portion of the Bunter in this neighbourhood. Only a few inches of this are exposed in the cutting.

Commencing with the northern face of the cutting at the western end, the first important feature is some large masses of sandstone, which have apparently been forced down into the marl as though by some heavy body passing above, the beds of marl being much contorted in their neighbourhood. Close to these are smaller masses of the same material broken off from the larger ones and embedded in the upper columnar marl. Further east are pockets of red sand, the grains of which are very much rounded (the above portion is not shown in the figure).

Then follows Boulder Clay (8), in a pocket underlying the Keuper Sandstone and embedded in the blue marl, also many

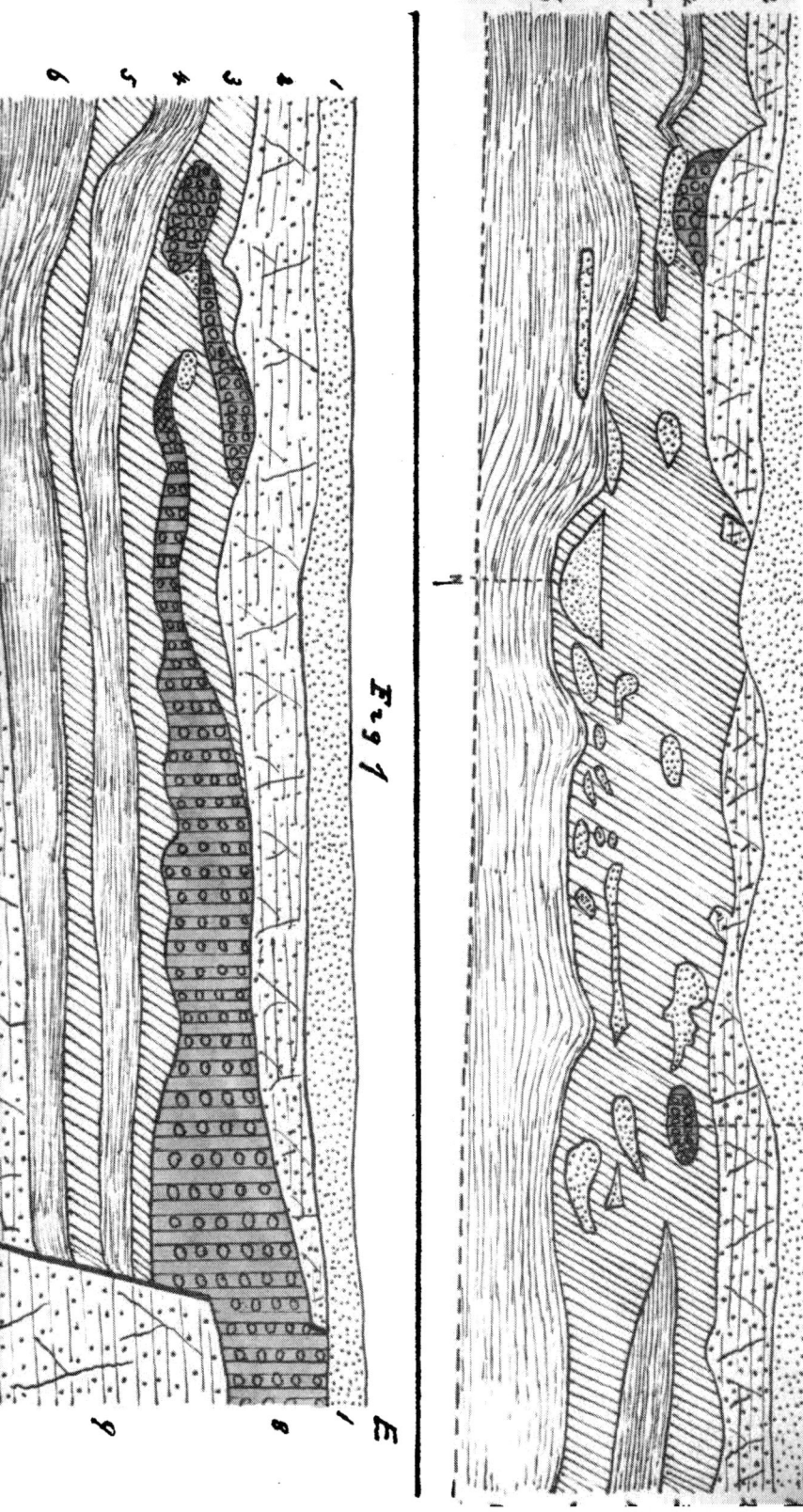

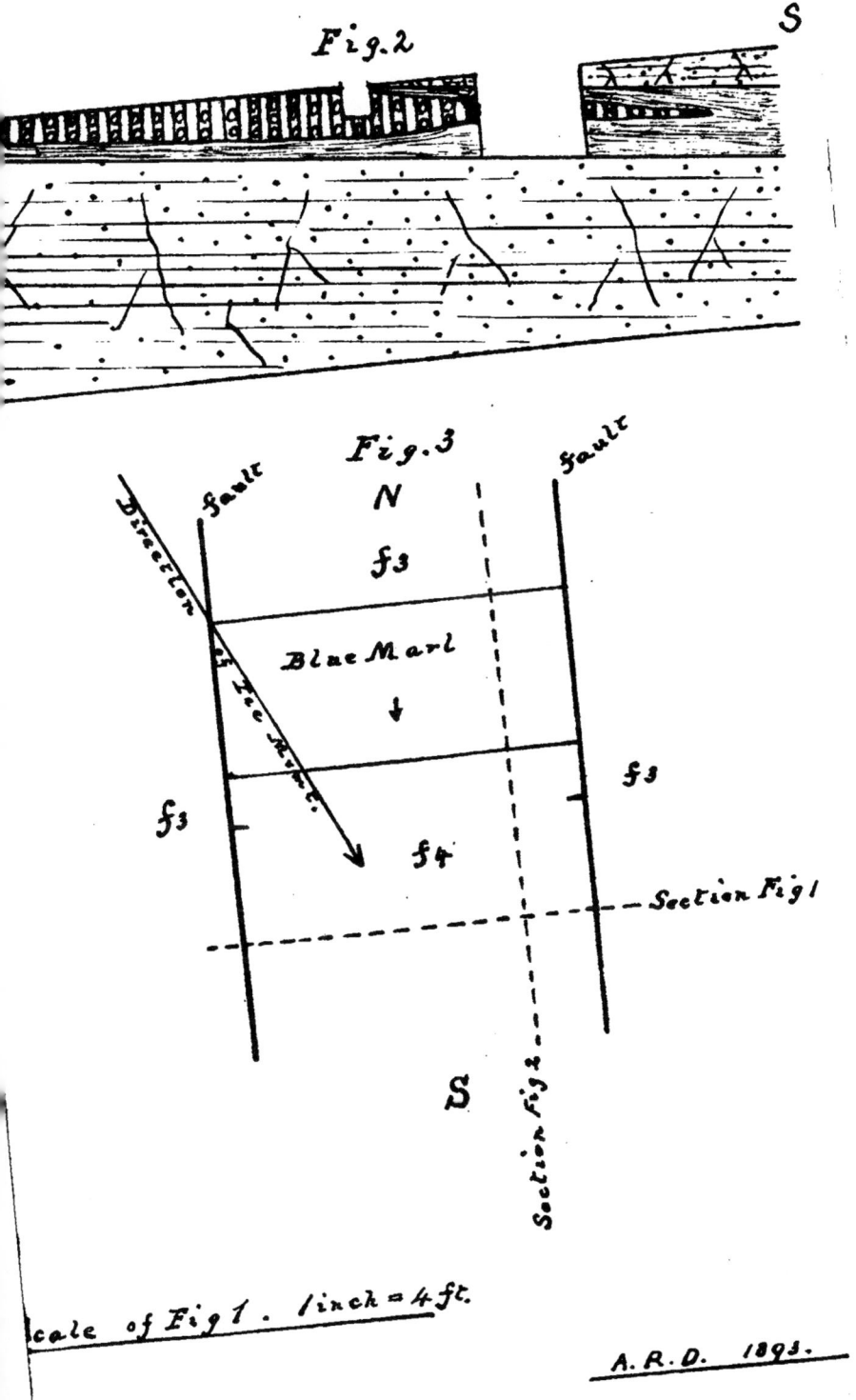

Scale of Fig 1. 1 inch = 4 ft.

A.R.D. 1893.

pockets of various coloured sand, all the grains being rounded as before. In this portion of the section the upper stratified marl appears to thin out, but in reality is so kneaded up with the upper and lower columnar beds as to be almost unrecognisable. At a point a few yards further east is another mass of Boulder Clay underlying the Keuper. Close to this the upper stratified marl again becomes well marked.

There are then two larger masses of Boulder Clay, with their accompanying sand pockets.

At the extreme east end of the section is a very large mass of Boulder Clay, underlying about two feet of Keuper Sandstone and a few inches of the upper columnar marl; the clay is forced close up to the face of the fault which cuts off the marl band.

The south face of the cutting is similar in most respects to the one already described, the most noticeable feature being a mass of Boulder Clay actually embedded in the Keuper Sandstone, that below the clay being much disturbed.

The marl band is much more regular on this, being further from the out-crop and protected by a thicker layer of sandstone overlying.

Fifty yards to the north of the main cutting was a smaller excavation, which showed the out-crop of the marl band, and still further north the Bunter appears on the surface (Figs. 2 & 3).

A section through the two excavations is given (Fig. 2), from which it will be seen that the Boulder Clay has been forced into the outcrop of the marl band underneath the Keuper Sandstone for a distance of at least fifty yards.

The sand from the pockets before referred to is exactly similar in colour, size of grain, and degree of roundness, to that of various beds of Bunter in the immediate neighbourhood, even a careful examination with the microscope failing to reveal any difference. From the above it is evident that the sand pockets were originally derived from the Bunter, and they must have found their way to their present position in one of two ways; either they were deposited contemporaneously with the marl, or they have been pushed in along with the Boulder Clay. I incline to the latter view inasmuch as the sand pockets are only found in the neighbourhood of the masses of

Boulder Clay, the parts of the section remote from these being free from sand pockets.

The Boulder Clay contained several well-scratched specimens of Andesite and Silurian Grit, also a few small masses of decomposed Granite containing white Felspars and black Mica, probably Scotch. The Boulder Clay is all at the eastern end of the section, and further, the beds of marl, so much contorted at this end, are at the west end comparatively undisturbed.

The explanation of the above is that the clay was introduced by an agent moving approximately from N.W. to S.E., the clay being thus forced against the face of the eastern fault, while the marl beds at the western end were undisturbed by reason of their being under the lee of the Bunter beyond the western fault (Fig. 3).

The finding of undoubted northern erratics shows that in this case we are dealing with glacial phenomena.

It is hard to see how, under submergence, floating ice would be capable of producing these effects. We must rather look for some agent producing a force from the N.N.W., and which was capable of moulding itself to the contour of the land.

The same direction is noticed in the glacial striæ, Crag and Tail, and other features which are found in the immediate neighbourhood, and it seems more reasonable to conclude that a great ice sheet has produced these effects, advancing from the N.N.W., passing along over the Bunter, and pushing portions of this together with Boulder Clay into the soft yielding marl band, grinding on over the harder Keuper, and in places where this was sufficiently thin, squeezing masses of it down into the underlying marl.

Proceedings of the Glacialists' Association.

24th February, 1891.—A meeting was held at the rooms of the Stockport Society of Naturalists, St. Petersgate, Stockport, convened by a circular issued to a number of geologists in East Cheshire. The circular ran—

> East Cheshire Boulder Committee.
>
> Dear Sir,—A preliminary meeting will be held on Tuesday, 24th inst., at 7.30 p.m., in the rooms of the Stockport Society of Naturalists, St. Petersgate. Your attendance is particularly requested.
>
> Yours faithfully, PERCY F. KENDALL.

Twenty gentlemen attended, and it was agreed, on the motion of Mr. C. E. DeRance, F.G.S., to form a society to be called the "North-West of England Boulder Committee," and that it should report periodically to Dr. Crosskey, as secretary of the Erratic Blocks Committee of the British Association, upon all boulders found by the members. The following officers were elected:—Secretary, Mr. P. F. Kendall; Assistant-Secretary, Mr. Jesse Reeves; Treasurer, Mr. J. Joyce; Curator, Mr. E. Hewett.

Donations of one guinea each for the purchase of maps were promised by Mr. J. W. Gray, F.G.S., and Mr. Thomas Kay, J.P.

21st March, 1891.—At Stockport, C. E. DeRance, F.G.S., in the chair. The secretary stated that in response to a second circular sent out, eleven gentlemen had joined the Society. A sub-committee was appointed to draw up a series of suggestions to aid members in dealing with miscellaneous glacial observations. It was agreed that the committee should meet monthly to receive and discuss papers, and that the meetings should be held at any place within the area of operations of the Society.

Messrs. Wakefield and Kendall promised donations of maps, and Mr. Kendall presented a large series of shells from the Drift deposits about Liverpool.

18th April, 1891.—At Stockport, Mr. C. E. DeRance in the chair. The secretary announced the accession of 17 new members. The following donations were also announced:—Sir Henry Fox Bristowe, Q.C., £1 1s. 0d., Mr. W. Brockbank, F.L.S., F.G.S., £1 1s. 0d. to the funds of the committee; the Director-General of the Geological Survey, 19 one inch maps; Mr. T. Axon and Mr. P. F. Kendall, a large series of rock specimens, chiefly granites, from Galloway; Mr. P. F. Kendall, a series of rock specimens from the Isle of Man and North Wales, and a specimen of the Ophicalcite, found on the Manchester Ship Canal at Barton. The thanks of the Society were accorded the donors.

A paper was read by the secretary, in the absence of the author, the Rev. C. R. Barker, B.A., "On some erratics from Stonyhurst, near Whalley, Lancashire." [The substance of this paper has appeared in the 19th Report of the Erratic Blocks Committee.]

Boulders were reported as follow, by :—

J. W. Gray, at Stockport; G. Shaw, at Bramall; C. E. DeRance, at Northern Etchells and Barton, Lanc.; E. Hewett, at Marple Dale; A. Taylor, at Offerton.

9th May, 1891.—At Stockport, Mr. C. E. De Rance in the chair. The secretary announced the accession of eight new members. The secretary submitted the draft rules, which were adopted subject to revision by the next meeting.

Members were nominated to fill the various offices.

A discussion took place on the preparation of a bibliography of British Glacial Geology, and Messrs. De Rance, Hewett, Kendall, and Lomas agreed to co-operate.

13th June, 1891.—At the University College, Liverpool, Mr. W. Hewitt, B.Sc., in the chair. The secretary announced the accession of seven new members. The draft rules adopted at the previous meeting were revised and adopted with slight modification. The election of officers then took place, with the following results:—

PRESIDENT, C. E. De Rance, F.G.S., etc., of H.M. Geol. Surv.; SECRETARY, P. F. Kendall, F.G.S.; ASSIST. SEC., Jesse Reeves; TREASURER, J. Joyce; CURATOR, E. Hewett; COUNCIL:—J. W. Gray, F.G.S, *Stockport;* C. Ricketts, M.D., F.G.S., *Birkenhead;* John Dale, *Macclesfield;* J. H. Grundy, *Ashton-under-Lyne;* G. J C. Broom, F.G.S., *St. Helens;* J. Tonge, F.G.S., etc., *Bolton;* Major John Plant, F.G.S., *Salford;* Bernard Hobson, M.Sc., F.G.S., *Manchester;* J. Lomas, A.N.S.S., *Liverpool;* T. Hart, F.G.S., *Grange-over-Sands;* W. L. Hind, M.D., F.G.S., *Stoke-upon-Trent;* W. Hampton, F.C.S., *Hanley;* Rev. C. R. Barker, B.A., *St. Asaph;* P. M. C. Kermode and Rev. S. N. Harrison, *Ramsey, I. of Man.*

Mr. J. Lomas, A.N.S.S., read a paper "On a newly discovered striated surface at Birkenhead." The secretary exhibited a series of boulders sent from Hest Bank by Mr. T. Ransome. He pointed out that they were all such rocks as occur *in situ* in the country draining into Morecambe Bay.

Mr. Kendall described three sections in the Drift near Stockport.

Review.

THE GLACIAL NIGHTMARE AND THE FLOOD: A second appeal to common sense from the extravagance of some recent Geology. By Sir HENRY H. HOWORTH, K.C.I.E., M.P., F.G.S., &c. 2 Vols., 8vo., pp. XXVII., 895 pp. London: SAMPSON LOW, MARSTON, & COMP.

Sir Henry Howorth has produced a book such, perhaps, as no other man could have written. His powers of literary research are, perhaps, without equal amongst English writers upon geological topics. In every book or article from his pen the fact is patent, and there is not one from which the best-read geologist may not learn. As a dialectician, too, the author has a mastery of vigorous and cogent argument that has often put to confusion adversaries of the first rank.

In the book before me these qualities are fully displayed, and the result is a work which, however widely we may differ from the author in his conclusions, must find a place on the book-shelf of every geologist who would be acquainted with the pros and cons of one of the most fiercely contested questions in the whole range of geological polemics.

Whoever would have a sheaf of apposite facts bound up with a telling argument to discharge at a theory, will find them here ready to his hand, no matter which side he take in the great controversy. If he have a penchant for land-ice he can select from the armoury the deadliest of weapons wherewith to assail "the Great submergence"; while, if his fancy lightly turn to icebergs, here he shall find a shaft to pierce the harness of the most hardened glacialist; or, finally, if neither ice afloat nor ice ashore find favour in his sight, he may find the weapon for a triangular duel with the two.

The task which the author has set himself is an onerous one— no less than to show that the " glacial phenomena" of the Northern Hemisphere are separable under two categories, one including the actual work of *valley-glaciers*, while the other series has been the product of a great "Flood," which has swept the area marked by the limits of the great drift deposits of Northern Europe and North America east of the Rocky Mountains.

How much is to be ascribed to each is not easy to discover from the book, and their relation in time is equally obscure; indeed, the confusion of, if not ideas, at least of *expression*, regarding the former of these questions is so profound that one may well despair of a solution. To cite an instance. " In North Wales the great mountain bosses of Snowdonia were no doubt the home of their own local glaciers, a fact which I do not know that any one disputes. The glaciers were the distributors of *débris* in various directions, and notably in the English Midlands" (p. 752). Our author has no objection to "local glaciers" which could extend from Snowdonia across Wales, the broad hollow of the Vale of Severn, and strand their erratics on the Lickey Hills at an altitude of 900 feet above sea-level, and *in boulder-clay, too*—a fact that ill accords with the elaborate arguments later against the glacial origin of boulder-clay; but that the Irish Sea was ever obstructed by the influx of glaciers, or that the Shap erratics were carried by ice across the Vale of Eden and over the Pennine Chain into Yorkshire he holds to be the sort of stuff that dreams—nightmares—are made of.

Such contradictions and confusions abound in all save the purely historical parts of the book. We frequently find an early paper of some author quoted to attest some fact, and in another place a later work either of the same or some other writer giving a direct negative to it, or even the error may be more modern than its refutation; for example, on page 85 we find an account of a paper by Professor Phillips, dated 7th November, 1826, describing the occurrence of boulders of Shap granite in the Lune, south of Lancaster at a locality a mile south of Carlisle, and at many places in Yorkshire; again (p. 190), Dr. Buckland, in his memorable paper in 1840, speaks of the dispersal of Shap boulders north-east and south; on p. 746 Mr. Goodchild, and on 747 Professor Harkness, are quoted for a similar distribution of Shap erratics; yet on p. 750 Mr. Mellard Reade is quoted for the astounding statement and inference " No Shap Fell granite has ever been found by me; nor have I ever heard of its having been found on the west side of the Pennine Chain—another fact proving that the erratic rocks of the area under consideration are confined to the drainage basin of the Irish sea. This fact seems to me fatal to the idea of an ice-sheet over-riding the great water-sheds, and points to a system of glaciers radiating from mountain nuclei". Of course it would be unjust to hold Sir Henry Howorth responsible for Mr. Reade's unfamiliarity with the bibliography of the subject upon which he is writing, or for the error of supposing Shap Fell to be on the eastern side of the Pennine Chain ; but he cannot be exonerated from great carelessness in giving currency to statements contradictory of facts which must have been fully within his knowledge, as, saving Mr. Reade, they are in the knowledge of all who have ventured to write upon such topics.

It is easy to see how such blemishes have made their mark upon the work. Sir Henry Howorth is a great worker and a devoted public servant, and his book has been written in the intervals of an extremely busy life, and we all know that nothing is more inimical to clear and consecutive argument than the piece-meal method of writing. The last page of the preface would disarm a critic less impressed than the present writer, with value of the author's work and the heroic determination with which it has been accomplished, in spite of " health and eyesight having been equally uncertain ; " but there are surely even adversaries who would have read proof-sheets and prevented the appearance of nine " literals " on a single page.

While there is much to find fault with in the arrangement of the matter, yet some, perhaps most, of the chapters are excellent. The historical review which occupies the major part of the first volume displays the author at his best. The concise summaries of the views of all the great writers upon the " Diluvium " are admirable, and are calculated to open the eyes of some of the would-be originators of new views. The research manifested here is remarkable, and not the least of the uses of this book will be the acquaintance which it will give us with writers whose work has been veiled in undeserved obscurity.

Little less valuable are the chapters devoted to the Astronomical and Meteorological theories of the cause of the Glacial period, and to the discussion of the geological evidence regarding recurrent glacial and inter-glacial periods. Upon these questions the author expresses no hesitating opinions, indeed, throughout the book, when he recognises a spade he calls it by its name with the most refreshing directness In the discussion of inter-glacial periods a most important contribution is, for the first time, published. The substance of a letter, in which Mr. Clement Reid announces the discovery of common weeds of cultivation in the supposed interglacial deposits of Cowden Glen, Hailes Quarry, and Redhall. This recalls the remark of a distinguished geologist, that he should not be surprised to hear that a copy of the *Scotsman* had been found in the " Upper boulder-clay " of Hailes, and it confirms the supposition that the beds were not in place.

Ramsay's theory of the origin of fiords and lake-basins by glacier-erosion, is criticised, of course adversely, and the discussion may be commended to all who desire to gain a clear conception of the conditions of the problem.

When we turn to the discussion of the Drift phenomena in detail, the inadequacy of literary attainments however great, or bibliographical research however profound, to make amends for the lack of that training in the field which appears alone able to give the faculty of weighing geological evidence, becomes apparent. Sir Henry Howorth has been to the great shell-beds of Capell Backen, he has seen some modern glaciers, and has looked into the sand pits near Swinton, but all else he takes at second-hand, and, as I have shewn, he is not always fortunate in the choice of his authorities.

In the presentation of the facts relating to England, instead of a consecutive and coherent description of the facts and salient features of each natural area, with citations of the authors whose observations are relied upon, we are presented with a series of verbal quotations of isolated arguments from this author or from that, not always the most recent, and it is utterly impossible to obtain a connected account of either one set of phenomena or of one district.

Among the many writers quoted, one looks in vain for the name of Carvill Lewis, an omission surely inexcusable in view of the great mastery of the facts displayed by that brilliant generaliser, and of the impetus which he gave to glacial geology in this country.

Nine hundred pages of letterpress is a portentous achievement, but even that had better have extended a little rather than that statements should go unjustified, such as " As to the origin of kames there is now virtually one opinion only " (p. 789), which is followed by Kinahan's arguments in favour of their marine origin, and by more or less definite expressions of opinion from the writings of Lyell, Green, J. Geikie, Murchison, and others, from which no clear concensus can be extracted.

No mention is made of their parallelism with the striæ, nor of their relation to boulder transport ; neither is there any reference to the fact that Dr. Wright has seen kames in course of formation at the foot of the Muir glacier ; there is, however, some further reference to the subject on p. 861, where we are informed that "So far as the best judges agree" the kames, eskers, asar, etc., " are the result of the meeting of conflicting currents and masses of water," Sir Henry has his views as to who are the "best judges," and I have mine, but it is very strange that he withholds the preference from those who have seen the formation of kames.

A wholly unwarranted statement is that on p. 808—" Turning to America, we have first to face the fact of the scarcity of true moraines there." This assertion is supported by a statement by Dana, that there are no distinct terminal moraines *in New England* (for which he gives a good reason); a wholly irrelevant quotation from Ramsay! Another, equally irrelevant, by Desor! and a long quotation from Dana upon the subject of the stratified drift, and the marine deposits of the "Champlain period." Not one word about the magnificent series of moraines hundreds of miles in length, that have been mapped, figured, and described by a hundred able *American* geologists.

The treatment of the evidence of the shells or shell-fragments found in our drift deposits is marred by the failing so manifest in other places, the lack of personal familiarity with the subject, a want that results in several fallacious arguments. This is particularly noticeable in the case of negative evidence, which, even more than the positive evidence, should be up to date. Thus on p. 724, Robertson's remark that *Fusus Turtoni, Fusus Norvegicus,*

Fusus Berniciensis, and *Saxicava* (*Panopœa*) *Norvegica* have not been found on the western coasts of Scotland was true enough when he wrote it, but no longer holds good.

The chapter headed "The distribution of the Drift can only be explained by a great diluvial catastrophe," is the great constructive effort of the book, but of actual construction there is after all very little. Hopkins' views upon "great waves of translation," and Scott Russell upon the efficiency of waves as transmitters of power, are stated at length; then we are given illustrations of the work done by actual floods, and a review of some facts of American Drift-geology which the author accepts as proof of such a flood; but what we want, and what the author omits to give us, is a little information as to where this great flood took its origin, which way its currents travelled, and generally what it did and how it did it. In his concluding paragraph, the author claims for his theory—or perhaps he would modestly throw back the credit for it upon his master Murchison—that " it enables us to bring under one common law the phenomena presented by the biological and archæological records with a large body of facts presented by stratigraphical geology, and above all it enables us to solve a great problem without ignoring a single fact, without fencing with a single difficulty, and without having recourse to arguments and to logic which belong to other domains than that of science." Whether he has really achieved so much, and by such means, is matter for individual judgment.

The title is not happily chosen for a sober contribution to the stony science, but after perusal of the book everyone will be prepared to admit that it has a certain appropriateness.

Nightmares in truth there be but :—

> Which Pretender is, and which is King,
> God bless us all, that's quite another thing.

Percy F. Kendall.

Greenland.

Glacialists everywhere will await with great expectancy the return of Dr. Erick von Drygalski and his companions in September next, after more than a year's sojourn in West Greenland.

The expedition was sent out at the instance of the Berlin Geographical Society, and had for its objects the study of the Greenland glaciers and inland ice. There was no lack of funds or scientific instruments, the German Emperor himself giving 16,000 marks towards the necessary expenses.

A preliminary expedition was made in the summer of 1891 in order to find the most suitable places for a station, and to determine the best lines on which to carry out the work. The results of this preliminary survey are published (Proc. Geog. Soc., Berlin, 1891, 8, p. 445, and in "Gronland's Gletscher ünd Inlandeis," Berlin Geog. Soc., 1892).

The station chosen was in $70\frac{1}{2}°$ N. Lat., on a nunatak behind the Umanakfjord, and surrounded by the Greater and Lesser Karajak Glaciers.

Since their departure in May, 1892, letters and reports have been received from the explorers. These give brief records of the work done, and from their character we believe that most important results will follow, and our knowledge of the phenomena of great ice-sheets will be very much increased.

Drumlins.

Mr. Warren Upham has recently (*Amer. Geologist*, Dec., 1892) restated and amplified his well-known theory of the origin of drumlins.

He ascribes to them an origin depending upon variation in the relation of snow-fall to ablation, or the reduction of the surface of a glacier by melting or evaporation.

He shows how by ablation a quantity of "englacial" *debris* may become superficial, and he supposes that an additional sheet of ice may cover it up, when the differential flow of the upper and lower strata of ice will, as he supposes, draw into masses the intervening *debris*. As the ice-sheet progresses, the drumlin-forming layer will gradually approach the wasting front, and the mounds will settle down upon the ground. The subsequent movement of the upper layer of ice will give the final form to the mound, and an unequal settlement of the drumlin by the incomplete melting of the subjacent ice may produce the fissuring and faulting occasionally seen in drumlins.

The whole paper should be read by all who are interested in these curious hills, and if the explanation offered should not meet with full approval, it will at least be regarded as a carefully thought-out contribution to an exceedingly puzzling question.

It is worthy of note, though Mr. Upham does not mention the fact, that the belts of drumlins to which he more specifically alludes (those of New Hampshire and New York), are at right angles to the ice movement in those districts, and therefore in the position in which, according to his theory, they ought to occur.

Obituary.

We regret to announce the death of the Rev. H. H. Higgins, M.A., F.G.S., who has for upwards of half a century taken an active part in the scientific life of Liverpool. He was a member of the Glacialists' Association, and did good service to geology by securing the preservation of some fine local boulders in the grounds of the William Brown Museum.

His loss will be felt by the various Natural History Societies of Liverpool, at whose meetings he was until recently a regular attendant.

Hull Boulder Committee.

The geologists of Hull have organised a "Boulder Committee," similar to that appointed by the Yorkshire Naturalists' Union, which has done such valuable work in the past few years.

The intention of the Hull committee is to allot to each member a certain portion of Holderness to be thoroughly searched for erratics. Incidentally other glacial phenomena will come under observation, and it is reasonable to hope that the increase of interest in the prevailing formation which occupies a wide area in the district, will react to the advantage of the societies which have shown such laudable enterprise.

The British Association Committee on Erratic Blocks.

Has issued a special appeal to the "corresponding Societies" to aid in recording erratic blocks in the various parts of the country. It is hardly creditable to the societies which are admitted to the advantages of affiliation to the British Association, that so little has been done to further the objects of the oldest of its committees of research. The Yorkshire Naturalists' Union has, by its Boulder Committee, done excellent work for some years, and the Glacialists' Association has sent in a very large number of reports of erratics, and between them the 1892 report is divided, not another individual or organisation being represented.

Arctic Geology.

Sir H. H. Howorth, F.R.S., whose election as a Fellow of the Royal Society will, we believe, be hailed with satisfaction by all who are acquainted with his work in Glacial Geology, has a suggestive paper in the *Geological Magazine* for July, the main object of which is to show that there are no evidences of the Glacial Period, or rather of former severe conditions of glaciation, in the Arctic regions. Geologists will always be thankful to Sir Henry Howorth for the unwearied industry with which he gathers together facts from various recondite sources, and for the literary skill with which he presents them, and, if they find a fundamental difference of opinion remaining at the last as to the way in which the facts are to be interpreted, they will at least agree that light has been thrown upon the subject, and the cause of truth has been advanced.

The evidence from Iceland collected by Mr. Gould has been negatived in an unmistakable way by the recent observations of Dr. Grossmann, which we hope to publish in our next issue. Sir Henry Howorth falls into the common error of supposing that a Glacial Period must always mean an ice-cap. The *aiguilles* in Iceland and Spitzbergen are not inconsistent with glacial conditions of extreme severity having prevailed in those islands very recently.

The Date of the Extinction of the Mammoth.

Mr. Mark Stirrup responds with some spirit in the *Geological Magazine* for July, to the rejoinder of Sir Henry Howorth upon the subject of the geological date of the extinction of the Mammoth. Mr. Stirrup incidentally throws a doubt upon the much talked of Utznach and Durnten gravels, with the implication, apparently, that there has been an actual mechanical mixing of the contents of a Pre-glacial deposit with the remains of a Post-glacial fauna. So long as such doubts are possible it would be rash to attach much weight to the evidence these beds afford of Interglacial periods.

Current Glacial Bibliography.

American Journal of Science. Third Series, Vols. XLIV. & XLV., July, 1892—June, 1893.

VOL. XLIV.

1.—*A Hint with respect to the Origin of the Terraces in Glaciated Regions*, p. 59.—R. S. TARR.

The author has studied the behaviour of the Colorado River, and finds that in a portion of its course where it is liable to floods 50 feet above the normal level, it has produced three terraces simultaneously.

2.—*Occurrence of a Quartz Boulder in the Sharon Coal of North-Eastern Ohio*, p. 62.—E. ORTON.

All the boulders hitherto found in American coal seams have come from a single seam, the middle Kittatinny in Ohio, the largest being of 400 lbs. weight. They are all of a grey quartzite. The present example is from the lowest Sharon seam of the conglomerate coal measures. It is not a quartzite, but consists of *vein quartz*. It is not shaped by any water or glacial action, but is quite angular as if freshly broken from the parent mass.

3.—*The Gulf of Mexico as a measure of Isostasy*, p. 191.—W. J. McGEE.

Deals on p. 191 with changes of level during the different phases of the Glacial Period.

4.—*Glaciation in the Finger Lake region of New York*, p. 290.—D. F. LINCOLN.

Describes—(1) A belt of drumlins; (2) Character and contents of the Till, and other deposits showing how the boulders are derived from outcrops to the northward; (3) The pre-glacial drainage and the origin of the Lakes, and concludes that they were produced partly by glacial erosion and partly by unequal deposition of Drift.

5.—*Ueber den gegenwärtigen Stundpunkt unserer Kenntniss von dem Vorkommen fossiler Glacialpflanzen*, p. 336.—A. G. NATHORST.

A brief notice of this memoir dealing with the present state of our knowledge of Glacial-floras. *Bihang till svenska Vet.—Akad Handlingar Band*, 17, *Afd. III., No.* 5.

6.—*Pleistocene Geography. Distributions of the La Fayette formation*, p. 339.—W. J. MCGEE.

Title only of paper to American Association.

7.—*Submarine Valleys on continental slopes*, p. 339.—WARREN UPHAM.

Same as preceding.

8.—*Terminal Moraines in New England*, p. 340.—C. H. HITCHCOCK.

Same as preceding.

9.—*Notes bearing upon the changes of the Pre-glacial drainage of western Illinois and eastern Iowa*, p. 340.—F. LEVERETT.

Same as preceding.

10.—*Extra-morainic Drift in New Jersey*, p. 340.—A. A. WRIGHT.

Same as preceding.

11.—*Periodic Variation of Glaciers*, p. 342.—Prof. FOREL.

An abstract of a communication to *Nature*, 18th August, 1892.

12.—*Unity of the Glacial Epoch*, p. 351.—G. F. WRIGHT.

The paper is a comprehensive examination, the American evidence of "Inter-glacial periods." The author concludes in favour of the Unity of the Glacial Epoch.

13.—*On Shells of a Northern character in a dry salt lake near Eddy, New Mexico*, p. 427.—V. STERKI.

Title of a memoir in *Geol. Surv. of Texas*, 3rd Annual Report for 1891.

14.—*Temperature of the Circumpolar Region*, p. 430.—J. GIRARD.

Mention of a paper in *Bull. Soc. de Géographie de Paris*, 2nd *trimester*, 1892.

15.—*Glacial Pot-holes in California*, p. 453.—W. H. TURNER.

The author describes a number of pits in granite which he ascribes to the action of water connected with a glacier. He mentions some circumstances favourable to another view of their origin.

16.—*Pleistocene History of North-Eastern Iowa*, p. 500.—W. J. McGee.

Mentioned as part of the 11*th Annual Report of the Director of the U.S. Geol. Surv.*

VOL. XLV.

17.—*View of the Ice Age as one Glacial Epoch*, p. 70.—WARREN UPHAM.

Extract from the author's paper on the "Accumulation of Drumlins" in *Amer. Naturalist*, Dec., 1892, in which he expresses his belief in one great epoch of glaciation with oscillations of the ice front in Europe and in America, and that it owed its occurrence to great altitude of the land at the commencement of the Glacial period.

18.—*The Pleistocene History of North-Eastern Iowa*, p. 71.—W. J. McGee.

Notice of memoir in the 11th Report of the Director of the U.S. Geol. Surv., 1889-90. The author finds two well-defined moraines indicative of two ice invasions. Over nearly half the area loess covers both deposits, and in a small area only one. Above the older moraine deposit there is generally a bed of soil with sticks and timber indicating a forest growth intervening between the two moraines.

Most of the loess the author considers to have been deposited in a lake, Lake Hennepin, produced by the junction of two ice-lobes to south of the well known driftless area. The third invasion by the ice fell short of this territory.

19.—*Excavation by Glaciers*, p. 74.—Prof. BALTZER.

Notice of a paper in *Arch. Sciet. Nat. Geneva*, Nov. 15, 1892. Prof. Baltzer describes his preparations for investigating the "Erosive action of Glaciers" in the valley of the Grindelwald Glacier. He states that according to his examination the work of excavation is partly simple abrasion, and partly splintering or crushing, especially where limestone is the exposed rock. He has bored holes in the limestone at the most favourable spots. The Glacier is now commencing a new advance, and he hopes to get results in the course of two or three years.

20.—CHAMBERLIN on the *Glacial Period*, p. 74.

A mention of a deferred paper.

21.—*The Diversity of the Glacial Period*, p. 71.—T. C. CHAMBERLIN.

A reply to Prof. G. F. Wright (12), dealing exclusively with American evidence, and stating the author's conclusion of the four divisions of the drift south of the Great Lakes, now employed as a working hypothesis, two or more will stand as well sanctioned epochs, to whatever grade the others may be relegated by the fuller knowledge of the future.

22.—*Estimates of Geologic Time*, p. 215.—WARREN UPHAM.

Reviews the estimates of Kelvin, Haughton, Croll, Dana, and others. Suggests that the estimation of Post-glacial time may furnish our unit. Gives the estimates based upon—(1) The recession of waterfalls (Winchell and Gilbert); (2) Erosion of the sides of Lake Michigan, and deposition at the southern end (Andrews); (3) Filling in of kettle-holes and erosion of valleys by streams tributary to Lake Erie (G. F. Wright); (4) Denudation of limestone rocks in Yorkshire and North Wales (Mackintosh), and Quebec (Logan and Bell). Considers with Prestwich that 30,000—40,000 may have comprised Glacial and Post-glacial time together, and adds some arguments in favour of the theory of a continental uplift to account for the Glacial Period. Believes that man was contemporary with the ice-sheet in America.

23.—*Are there traces of Glacial Man in Ohio?* p. 335.—W. J. MCGEE.

Title of a paper in Vol. I., No. 1, of *The Journal of Geology*.

24.—*The Nature of the Englacial Drift of the Mississippi basin*, p. 355.— T. C. CHAMBERLIN.

Title of a paper in Vol. I., No. 1, *The Journal of Geology*.

25.—*On a Champlain (?) deposit of Diatomaceæ belonging to the Littoral Plain*, p. 385.—ARTHUR M. EDWARDS.

Describes, with list, fresh water, marine, and brackish Diatoms from Champlain (?) clays of Newark, N.Y.

26.—*Fossil Plants as a test of Climate*, p. 438.—A. C. SEWARD.

Brief notice of the Sedgwick prize essay.

27.—*Nitikin on the Quaternary deposits of Russia and their relation to Prehistoric Man*, p. 459.—A. A. WRIGHT.

A summary of the paper read at the International Congress of Archæology, Moscow, 1892, in which Nitikin discussed at length the theory of Interglacial periods. He rejected the three or four glacial periods of some authors, and declared that there was in Finland no proof of two glacial periods separated by an Interglacial period. If one accepted the latter sub-divisions it would seem that the second glaciation cannot have extended beyond a comparatively restricted part of the Baltic region.

He discusses the relation of man to the Glacial Period in Russia, and holds that the great accumulations of remains of mammoth and other great quadrupeds in Russia, are contemporaneous with the second glaciation, which also marks the earliest traces of man in Russia.

BALTZER, PROF., 19; CHAMBERLIN, T. C., 20, 21, 24; EDWARDS, A. M., 25; FOREL, O., 11; GIRARD, JULES, 14; HITCHCOCK, C. H., 8; HOLMES, W. H., 23; LEVERETT, F., 9; LINCOLN, D. F., 4; McGEE, W. J., 3, 6, 16, 18; NATHORST, A. G., 5; NITIKIN, 27; ORTON, E., 2; SEWARD, A. C., 26; STERKI, V., 13; TARR, R. S., 1; TURNER, H. W., 15; UPHAM, WARREN, 7, 17, 22; WRIGHT, A. A., 10, 27; WRIGHT, G. F., 12.

The July Meeting.

The July meeting of the Association was held on the 29th ult., at the Town Hall, Buxton, the President, Mr. C. E. De Rance, F G.S., etc., in the chair.

Miss L. Shipton, and Misses Hallam and A. Timmins, were elected members of the Association.

The following communications were read and discussed:—

(1) On the section of sands and gravels at Heck Station, by C. E. De Rance, F.G.S., etc.; (2) On the discovery of an equivalent of the Coombe-rock at Askern, near Doncaster, by Percy F. Kendall, F.G.S.; (3) On an intrusion of boulder-clay at Kinnerton, Cheshire, by Arthur R. Dwerryhouse; (4) On the discovery of erratics at Fairfield, Buxton, by Miss Elizabeth Dale.

Notice.

The next meeting of the Association will be held at the Technical School, Stockport, on Saturday, 26th August, 1893, at 4 P.M.

The following new members will be balloted for :— Miss Mitchell, Pembury Road, Lower Clapton, London ; and Mr. William Millett, 6, West Street, Buxton.

PAPER :—The granite boulders of the Clyde Valley, by Dugald Bell, F.G.S.

Printed by Libri Plureos GmbH in Hamburg, Germany